The
Mission
of the
Catholic
Family

On the Pathway to Heaven

Rick Sarkisian, Ph.D.

Basilica Press
San Diego

Copyright © 1999 Basilica Press

ISBN 0-89870-851-6

Cover design and illustrations by Jim Goold.

99 00 01 02 03 15 14 12 11 10 09 08 07 06 05 04 03 02 01

Printed in the United States of America

To the Holy Family
and to
My Family

Table of Contents

Acknowledgments

I am very grateful to my good friends Louis Markert and Timothy Messenger for their encouragement, support, and assistance as the book began to take shape and form.

Also, thanks to the Oblates of St. Joseph, especially my good cousin, Fr. Larry Toschi, OSJ, and Fr. Brian Crawford, OSJ, for their review of the manuscript.

The valuable assistance of Phebe Wahl for transcription and layout, and Jim Goold for original art work have added much to this work.

I am continually appreciative for the editorial comments of Christopher Knuffke and Michael Phillips and for the ongoing support of Patrick Madrid of Basilica Press.

Most of all, thanks to the daily inspiration that flows from my wife and five children, and for the powerful intercession of St. Joseph.

Rick Sarkisian, Ph.D.
March 19, 1999
Feast of St. Joseph

Introduction

The Journey Begins

Three Traveling Families

Once there were three families, each going on vacation. The first family packed up and headed out, but had no destination, no map, and no travel plan. They just drove.

The second family had a destination, but no map, and no real plan for getting there. They drove in the general direction of their destination.

The third family had a very specific destination, a map, and a plan. They watched the signs along the way and stayed on course.

❖ ❖ ❖

The first family never got anywhere. They went with the flow of traffic. They never reached a destination because they didn't have one. They even had a difficult time finding their way home.

The second family had a hard time getting to their destination. They often received wrong directions along the way. They got lost frequently. By the time they happened upon their destination, it was time to go home.

The third family made steady progress toward their destination, and had confidence they were taking the right roads. Signs every few miles told them so. They arrived at their destination exactly as they had planned.

The Path to Heaven

Heaven is the ultimate destination for every family because it is perfect existence with the Holy Trinity, Mary and Joseph, the angels, and all those souls called there from this temporary, earthly home. It is the fulfillment of our permanent identity as children of God and the goal of human thoughts, words, and actions (*Catechism of the Catholic Church* [*CCC*] 2207).

Today, more than ever, families need a clear sense of purpose and direction. Your family needs to know where it is going and how to get there—not in terms of a favorite vacation spot, but to your ultimate spiritual destination, Heaven. By discovering your family's spiritual mission and purpose, then preparing a mission statement, you hold a road map to Heaven. Discovering your mission as a Catholic family is a means of staying on course and recognizing when corrections in the journey are necessary, so that you will get there.

God's Plan for the Family

The message in this book is two-fold: to discover God's plan for your family in terms of **IDENTITY** (what your family is all about in God's view) and **MISSION** (what your family can and should do) (*The Role of the Christian Family in the Modern World*, 17).

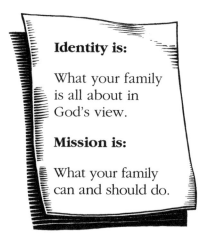

Identity is:

What your family is all about in God's view.

Mission is:

What your family can and should do.

God calls you to a general vocation to live a life of holiness and to a specific vocation or state of life such as marriage, priesthood, consecrated life, or single life.

He also calls you to a mission or purpose as a general witness to others of Jesus Christ and specifically to using God-given talents to bring glory to God in every activity (as in work, home, school, parish, and community).

The vocation and mission of each family member becomes united under one roof, so that the family as a whole has a common purpose in response to God's call.

Family vocation is . . .

. . . the universal call to holiness and the specific call to marriage and family life.

Family mission is . . .

. . . the general witness to others of Christ's living presence in the home and the specific function or purpose of the family as part of God's plan.

The collective use of gifts and talents gives your family an **identity** as a Christian witness to others. Before we focus on the mission of today's Catholic family, let us first see how the Holy Family followed God's will.

✦ ✦ ✦

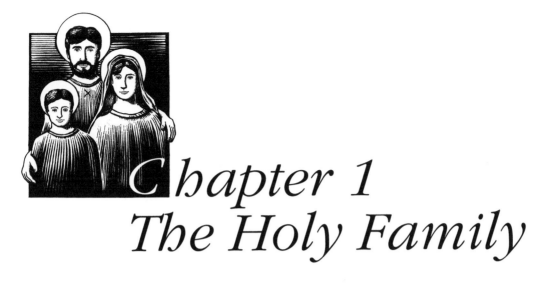

Chapter 1
The Holy Family

A Community of Life and Love

The Holy Family of Nazareth lovingly points to your destination—eternal life in Heaven. The individual lives of Jesus, Mary, and Joseph are clear reflections of their spiritual calling to a vocation and mission. They offer rich insight into God's view of the family. They are a model of family life full of beauty, truth, and goodness. They provide fulfillment of Gods words:

"For I know the plans I have for you, says the Lord, plans for welfare and not for evil, to give you a future and a hope. Then you will call upon me and come and pray to me, and I will hear you. You will seek me; and find me when you seek me with all your heart." Jeremiah 29:11–13

In one sense, the Holy Family is a united, earthly trinity, reflecting the Holy Trinity in Heaven. Likewise, the Christian family is a communion of persons, and a sign of the communion of Father and Son in the Holy Spirit (*CCC* 2205).

The Holy Family was united with Heaven at the birth of Jesus, and shared in the normal, day-to-day activities common to families of that time. There were struggles, to be sure, such as the urgent flight to Egypt during Herod's persecution, or Rome's continued oppression of the Jews. Yet this family ate, talked, prayed, worked, laughed, traveled, and grew together. They were a reflection of God's plan for family togetherness.

God was at the center of their home and at the center of their individual lives. Obedience and humility were particularly evident, such as Mary and Joseph's acceptance of God's plan to be parents of the Messiah and their continuing surrender to God's will after the birth of Jesus. Joseph and Mary were Holy Spouses united in common faith and acceptance of God's will, regardless of the circumstances or outcome. For example, their "yes" to God the Father is clear when Joseph took his family in the night to Egypt, and when Mary stood as a witness to her son's crucifixion.

Their mission and **your** mission share the **same path** (although the scenery may be different) and the **same hope**—the resurrected life in eternal worship of God in Heaven, your true home and destination (*CCC* 2233).

Your family also provides the setting for individuals to discover and follow God's plan for their personal vocation and mission. The members of the Holy Family are clear portraits of how this takes place, particularly in following God's will and living out the role of father, mother, and

child during the earthly journey toward Heaven.

✦ ✦ ✦

Joseph is a model for husbands and fathers in this age.

Joseph—Guardian of the Redeemer

Joseph was protector of the Holy Family. He is also protector of the Church, and is thus protector of the family—the domestic church. He responded to God's call with great humility and obedience. As a family man, his life was spent working, praying, and living in support of Jesus and Mary. He is an incredible example of one who followed God's plan in marriage, family, and work. This was his unique, personal vocation and mission. Joseph responded, like Mary, to the will of God the Father and His divine plan. God has a very personal vocation and mission for you, too.

Long before the "Lord's Prayer," Joseph was a living, breathing example of what "Thy will be done" really means. Mary and her child were entrusted to Joseph's care and fatherhood within their home, and he provided the foundation for Jesus' early growth and maturity.

Joseph, as quiet servant to God Almighty, was raised to a great destiny, reminding us that we need authentic virtues and character strengths to be faithful followers of Christ (*Guardian of the Redeemer*, 24). He was an ordinary, devout, hard-working young man chosen by God among all men to be father to Jesus.

Joseph is a model for husbands and fathers in this age. He understood the importance of placing God in supreme position at the center of his life and in Kingship over his family. He cooperated with God's will in living out his vocation and mission, ever obedient to God's presence and unfolding plan. He was devoted in love and sacrifice to Mary, and took great care in providing a secure setting for their growing Son, Jesus. There is no greater earthly example for fatherhood than Joseph.

Mary—Mother of the Redeemer

Mary, mother of Jesus, is also Mother of the Church and queen of families—the domestic church. She points the way to Jesus, and with her spouse, Joseph, guides parents along the path of holiness in marriage and family life.

Mary was united with Joseph in a common vocation, consecrated to God and each other in marriage, and in creating a home that would be suitable for the growth and development of God's Son.

Mary is a beautiful example of motherhood, humility, and holiness.

Through her mission, you are given a sign post along the road to salvation. She wants you to find her Son and bring Him fully into your heart and home, just as she brought Him into her own heart and home at Nazareth.

Mary is a beautiful example of motherhood and of complete fidelity to her spouse. She was filled with humility and sought God's presence in all she did. In some ways, her life was quite ordinary, yet she rose to extraordinary holiness. It is in the simple day-to-day events of home life that Mary shines as a model of simplicity, as well as love for her husband and child.

Jesus—The Redeemer

Jesus, true God and true man, was at the very center of life within the Holy Family (*CCC* 1655). His entire mission was to bring salvation, creating the pathway and signs that point to Heaven. He is a rock solid foundation for families and wants to be at the very heart of family life.

Jesus leads the family to salvation.

When He established His Church, He established a body of followers that could carry His mission and message of redemption to "the ends of the earth." This, then, is the mission of the Church and of all members of the Church that He calls to Himself. Families, of course, make up in large numbers that body of believers, and therefore share a major role in the mission of evangelization—bringing the Gospel message to all people.

The Church, like Christ, is mainly concerned with souls and a person's salvation. Families should be concerned as well about matters of the soul and salvation for each family member. All activity should support this end. Building a family life of prayer through the seasons of the Church is a safeguard against the moral decay of this world.

By placing Jesus at the center of your family and embracing His mission of salvation as your own, then your family is well-positioned on the right path— one that will bring you to God and bear much fruit along the way.

Jesus is also a wonderful example to children, especially in His youth as He remained obedient to God and to His earthly parents. Like other children of His time, Jesus played, learned Scripture, and probably enjoyed family discussion about faith and other important issues. He had such discussions as a young boy in the temple, and in adult life with believers and nonbelievers. In His youth, Jesus was absorbed into the Jewish culture and beliefs that were part of His home and the community of Nazareth. Like Jesus, today's children can be absorbed into a religious culture within the home, growing in faith and understanding of what it means to be a Catholic (*CCC* 1656).

Jesus not only helps families build their domestic church, He also offers original "designs" for each family. He provides a blueprint with construction details, so that you can build your family in a way that is consistent with God's plan. Your role as a family is to gain knowledge of God's purpose (family mission) and to follow the plan with faithfulness.

The Holy Family for Today

On the family's journey to the Father, we must not overlook the importance of Mary and Joseph as timeless teachers for our role as parents. As chosen father of Jesus, St. Joseph revealed the mercy and love of God the Father in his home. Fathers today must also reveal the mercy, forgiveness, and compassion of our God, especially since fathers are usually the first experience of God's paternity to children. St. Joseph is a man who reflects holiness in his simplicity, hard work, and dedication to his God and his family. He is at the heart of the salvation message.

Joseph taught Jesus important lessons about life, as we must do with our children. Fathers must teach their sons (and daughters) about the meaning of authentic manhood and mothers must instruct their daughters (and sons) about authentic womanhood. If parents don't get involved with their children's voyage into adulthood, then, by default, the world gets involved. All kinds of distorted images follow, dumped on our kids by TV, movies, magazines, sports, and other media figures that pitch superficial images of masculinity and femininity.

We must turn our children away from contemporary political and secular agendas that attempt to shape who we should be as men and women, and instead turn our attention to Joseph and Mary. What better examples are there? If Joseph and Mary were good enough for Jesus, they're good enough for us.

Summary

The Holy Family of Nazareth is a portrait of family life that is to be studied and lived. God had a unique vocation and mission for Joseph and Mary as he does for each family. When we develop a devotion to the Holy Family, we place our trust in Jesus, Mary, and Joseph and enter the core of the salvation message. The path of holiness they offer takes us straight to Heaven. Creating a Catholic culture in our homes becomes the daily expression of faith in God and the eternal life that awaits us.

✦ ✦ ✦

Prayer to the Holy Family
(Pope Paul VI)

Holy Family of Nazareth, teach us to be spiritually aware of your presence, and give us the sensitivity to heed the words and inspirations of true teachers. Make us conscious of our need to form ourselves through study, through a personal interior life, and through a hidden life of prayer known only to God. Show us what it means to be family, a Communion of love, in simple and plain beauty, with a sacred and inviolable nature. Amen.

✦ ✦ ✦

Chapter 2
The Mission

Discovering God's Plan for Your Family

What Is a Mission?

A mission usually involves a specific purpose or task. For your family, it is God's call to what you can and should do as members of His Kingdom on earth.

The Role of the Christian Family

Pope John Paul II published his Apostolic Exhortation *Familiaris Consortio* (*The Role of the Christian Family in the Modern World*) in November 1981, summarizing the developments from the 1980 Bishops Synod on the Family in the Modern World.

The Pope writes about God's plan for marriage and family, the role of the Christian family, the pastoral care of family, and many other family topics.

The family's mission is to become more and more of what it is—a community of life and love, on the journey to fulfillment in the Kingdom of God (*The Role of the Christian Family in the Modern World*, 17).

The mission of the family is also to **guard, reveal, and communicate love,** which reflects God's love for His people and Christ's love for His Church.

Four Tasks of the Family

At the Synod, four general tasks of the family were emphasized.

1. Forming a Community of Persons

All family members, each according to their individual gifts, have the grace and responsibility of building, day-by-day, richer spiritual bonds with each other. It is a life of love between spouses and through the entire family, including extended members (*The Role of the Christian Family in the Modern World*, 18–27).

2. Serving Life

This includes the transmission of life, along with the primary vocation of married couples to educate their children in those areas necessary for being a mature Christian. Education in the virtue of chastity is absolutely essential here (*The Role of the Christian Family in the Modern World*, 28–41).

3. Participating in the Development of Society

The family is seen as the first and vital cell of society. Families should be especially mindful of the poor and disadvantaged in living out their mission (*The Role of the Christian Family in the Modern World*, 42–48).

4. Sharing in the Life and Mission of the Church

The family functions as a believing and evangelizing community, in dialogue with God, at the service of man. Parents must teach their children to pray, with emphasis on devotional practices promoted by the Church, particularly devotion to the Sacred Heart of Jesus and devotion to Mary, especially through the Rosary. (*The Role of the Christian Family in the Modern World*, 49–64).

These tasks apply to all Catholic families. However, your family also has a unique identity and mission to discover as your own. Even among religious orders and communities, the common mission of evangelization is shared. Yet each order has a distinct mission that becomes part of its religious life, such as teaching, nursing, or working with the poor.

Your family must be a community of life and love in your home, society, and church. Your family mission statement provides structure for living God's plan in each of these areas.

What Is a Mission Statement?

A mission statement is a brief, yet clear summary of your family's purpose as members of God's larger, extended family—the Church. It provides an easily understood definition of what your family is all about and what you **can** and **should be** according to God's design. The mission statement creates a view of where your family is heading as you live out your vocation. In written form, it becomes a road map for the family's earthly pilgrimage to God the Father.

Why Have a Mission Statement?

Imagine a country without a constitution or a sporting event without rules. How about a corporation without policies or a college without a philosophy? Without such guidelines, chaos can result. Your family without a statement of purpose and mission leaves much to be assumed or implied as to who you are and where you are heading. Failing to discover your family mission means that you have no well-defined purpose. The doors are wide open for society and its self-serving values to dictate purpose for you, leaving your family very vulnerable. A mission statement defines a purpose for living

and maps a spiritual course for life's travels on the path to Heaven. It applies to all kinds of families, including married couples with or without children, families with older or adult children (including "empty nesters"), grandparents, and single parents. In fact, an extended family mission statement that includes grandparents is a strong definition of common identity in Christ.

The Mission of the Catholic Family

Preparing a mission statement is much like planning a long journey. The most important part of the journey is to know your destination (see chapter 5). Once you know where you are going, then you can plan the trip, pack the suitcase, and take off. A cross-country trip begins with a good look at road maps and knowing which highways, exits, and city streets will lead you to your final destination. Without a map, you are likely to get lost. The map gives you a reference point for staying on course and lets you know if corrections should be made. After all, you may not always stay on course and may need to make adjustments to avoid straying too far from the desired route. Your mission statement is your family's map for the journey.

Traffic engineers know that the typical driver does not travel or "track" down the road in a straight path, but rather weaves back and forth a few inches, while remaining within the traffic lane.

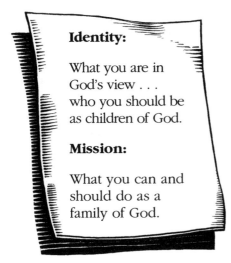

Identity:

What you are in God's view . . . who you should be as children of God.

Mission:

What you can and should do as a family of God.

Such is family life, so that even with a mission statement in place, adjustments are necessary while you remain within your spiritual lane. A statement about your family mission guides you within that lane and is a means of knowing whether or not you have strayed too far.

The absence of a mission statement leaves your family on a multilane freeway with no lane dividers and no destination, subject to the flow of traffic and the idiosyncrasies of other drivers, similar to the way families are being influenced by societal pres-

sures, media culture, and materialism. Detours are commonplace and the lack of a mission statement makes it much easier for society to create your identity. Sure, you are not forced to listen to society, but it is all too easy to let the "modern world" fill the vacuum in the lives of individual family members, or the empty spots in your family as a whole. Your family, through God's will and grace, learns true identity and purpose.

Creating Your Mission Statement

Your family mission statement is developed and put to use by going through four steps:

1—Defining the current state of your family.
2—Planning your mission statement.
3—Preparing your mission statement.
4—Using your mission statement.

Family discussions and prayer serve to shape and form your mission statement, and are crucial to creating a vision for your family. Done weekly before, during, and after your mission statement is developed, family talks are a powerful way to foster greater unity among parents and children. A typical family discussion may last 30 to 60 minutes and includes:

1. Gathering together.
2. Opening with prayer.
3. Discussion among family members regarding a specific topic or theme related to family mission (such as current state of your family).
4. Summarizing the discussion.
5. Closing with prayer.

Of course, family discussions can also be spontaneous and may take place whenever the need arises.

Step 1—Defining the Current State of Your Family

The first step toward developing a mission statement for your family is to take a good look at what your family is like now. Although this may not be your true family identity desired by God in His plan, it is an identity that defines the present situation, and gives a baseline reading, showing what needs work.

Discussions about your family's current state should occur with all members present. A designated "note-taker" should record the important elements of the dis-

cussion. These discussions should occur at least weekly on a consistent basis so that progress can be made toward discovering identity and mission as a Catholic family.

Following is a list of suggested topics for these get-togethers. Use these topics to encourage every member to talk about their view of your family. Certain family members may not want to talk much or at all. Encourage their participation and, at the very least, make sure they are present. Be sure to begin and end each family discussion with prayer.

Suggested Themes

What Our Family Is About Now

+ What kind of family are we?
+ What do we enjoy doing together?
+ When do we get along best?
+ What is most important to me (us) in our family?
+ How do we express ourselves spiritually as a family?
+ Do we offer love (charity) in the community around us?
+ Do we each have specific and clear responsibilities in the home?

◆ How is Christ present in our family?

◆ For each person, describe what you like most about your family? . . . Like least?

◆ What are the special talents and abilities present in each of us?

◆ What is most important spiritually to our family?

◆ How do we serve the Church?

It may be possible to understand what your family is like in only one or two meetings, or with just a few questions. Some families may take a longer period of time to gain an understanding of their present state. The important thing is to keep talking and have regular meetings, even if several weeks or longer pass before a good understanding results.

Once your family completes this first step and understands the current state, then you are ready to consider how God views your family's true identity.

Step 2—Planning Your Mission Statement

How can your family be an image to the community as a loving, vibrant unit filled with the desire to mirror Christ? You can do this by seeking God's will and purpose, and by adhering to a well-developed mission statement. In discovering the purpose of your family and defining a common mission, your family achieves true identity as a Christian family.

Planning your mission statement is the discovery of God's plan for your family—what you **can** and **should be**—a community of life, love, faith, and hope, in service to the Church. Your family mission statement is a written expression of His plan.

The process of developing your mission statement begins with emphasizing a strong sense of purpose, knowing where you want to go, and how to get there as a family. Your mission statement provides the road map for getting to Heaven. Discovering God's special plan for your family will normally involve prayer and additional family discussions. Some suggestions follow:

Suggested Themes
for Family Discussions

◆ What does God want of us right now?

◆ What does God want us to be?

◆ What does God want us to do?

- How can we be more Christ-like to each other? To others in the community?
- How can we be more like the Holy Family?
- How can we be more loving to each other?
- How can we improve our service within the Church and community?
- What virtues should symbolize our family's purpose (such as faith, hope, charity, kindness, temperance, compassion, work, courtesy)?
- How should we address problems or difficulties in the family?
- What should be most important to our family?
- How can we pray together as a family?
- How can we share our faith with others?
- What is our family's vision for the future in our home? In Church? In society?

Family discussions can be an exciting time for coming together in new ways; looking at where you have been, where you are, and where you want to be. Here are some specific activities for parents and children to strengthen the family and to open the door for the gift of increased faith.

What Parents Can Do

- Develop an awareness of your own vocation and mission. How is God calling you personally? Share this with your spouse and children.
- Encourage discussion among family members regarding what is important to each person.
- Serve as an example of Christ's presence in the home. (Children **do** see us as we are, not how we would "like" to be seen.)
- Pray with children at the beginning and end of each family discussion.
- Foster a deep awareness that each family member has a unique, personal vocation and mission . . . a special plan, designed by God for each person. Identify and discuss the God-given talents and gifts within yourself and your children.
- Educate your children in timeless and important virtues of life—especially the virtues found within the Holy Family.

+ Encourage discussion about what your children value most.

+ Provide a secure place for character development and virtue formation. Make your home a classroom of love, kindness, and forgiveness.

+ Give a solid foundation in the Catholic faith: what we believe and how we live it. Develop a regular in-home program of religious instruction.

+ Frequently refer to your family mission statement, making "course corrections" if necessary.

+ Gather often around a family home altar for prayer.

What Children Can Do

+ Take an active role in developing your family mission statement. Contribute as much as possible to family discussions.

+ Pray daily about your family's mission.

+ Find positive qualities about those within your family, then tell them.

+ Think about the family events that make you happy, and share your thoughts with your parents.

+ Describe your most memorable family activities.

+ Consider what your responsibilities are in the home and discuss your thoughts with your parents.

+ Consider ways your family can improve.

+ Ask God to show you His plan for your life.

+ Place Jesus first in your life.

+ Talk with your parents about God. How is He present in your life?

+ Read Sirach 3:2–6.

Step 3—Preparing Your Mission Statement

Your family mission statement should represent a mixture of ideas gained in family conferences, not a parental proclamation to the children. It is a result of a collaborative, consultative, prayerful process. The ideas expressed are blended together and poured out into a single cup that will contain a statement of who you are as a family (family identity in God's plan) and what you can accomplish for God's Kingdom (family mission and purpose).

Qualities of a Good Mission Statement

1. Brief and defines the family's vision, purpose, and desired virtues.
2. Clear to all who read it.
3. Placed in a prominent location within the home.
4. Discussed at least weekly in family meetings.

Your mission statement should be developed with a specific emphasis on what your family can do in three areas:

Home: In the home, an emphasis is placed on your family as a community of life and love.

Society: In society, your family is particularly aware of helping the poor and disadvantaged, physically and spiritually, and of joining other families in common Catholic faith.

Church: In the Church, your family embraces its role as a church in miniature, with special devotion to prayer.

A worksheet is offered at the end of this chapter to help your family prepare a mission statement. Some opening statements for your family's mission statement might be:

"As a community of life and love, we are . . ."
"In the world around us, we will . . ."
"In sharing in the life of the Church, we shall . . ."

or

"In our family, we . . ."
"In our community, we . . ."
"In our Church, we . . ."

or

"As a family of life and love . . ."
"In society, we . . ."
"In service to Christ's Church . . ."

A blank family mission statement is provided at the end of this book. It should be prepared, mutually agreed upon, signed, and used by your family as a spiritual map and travel itinerary.

It is important that each member be involved in creating your family mission statement. Thus, everyone has ownership of it, including young children, as well as teenagers seeking their own independence.

Examples:

The following examples of family mission statements are provided to guide you in preparing your family mission statement.

Here is an example of a completed family mission statement:

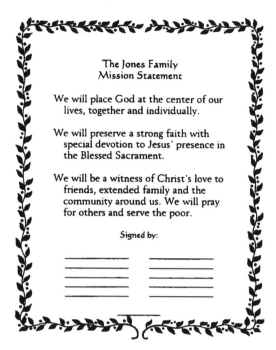

The Jones Family
Mission Statement

We will place God at the center of our lives, together and individually.

We will preserve a strong faith with special devotion to Jesus' presence in the Blessed Sacrament.

We will be a witness of Christ's love to friends, extended family and the community around us. We will pray for others and serve the poor.

Signed by:

And following the example of the Holy Family:

Family Mission Statement

We will keep God at the center of our home and individual lives and follow His Will in everything we do.

We will live a life worthy of the calling each has received, bringing glory to God in our thoughts, words, deeds and prayers.

Our lives will be devoted to cooperating with the mission of the Redeemer in whatever way God may ask.

Signed by:

Here is another example of a family mission statement with some key elements omitted:

The _____ Family
Mission Statement

As a community of life and love, we will activly seek to _____ _____ within our home and _____ within the community.

We will be a witness to God's love by _____ _____ in service to the Church.

We will place special emphasis on the virtues of _____, _____ and treat each other with _____.

Signed by:

The more personal and concrete your mission statement, the better. There may be some further refinement as you use the mission statement, but eventually your family should reach a point where it is time to make the mission statement formal. There should be a special family event when this occurs. Here is a guideline for putting your family mission statement into action.

A Simple Ceremony

+ Gather around a table or home altar with a large, center candle and an individual candle for each family member.
+ Light the large center candle.
+ Offer an opening prayer and Scripture reading (for example, Joshua 24:14–15, Deuteronomy 6:5, I Timothy 3:4–5).
+ Parents express appreciation for the children's contributions in developing the mission statement.
+ Read the mission statement aloud (one person or all present).
+ Sign the mission statement, one by one, lighting a candle from the large center candle each time.
+ Close with prayer, then enjoy a special family meal or other activity commemorating the event.

By a simple ritual, your family underscores the importance of your mission statement as a written proclamation of their faith in God.

Step 4—Using Your Mission Statement

Your family mission statement is a powerful tool for uniting your family with a common purpose and direction. It is like an old compass I have, made in 1917, that has never failed to point north. The mission statement is your spiritual compass. It points you toward God and your heavenly home, and gives you feedback when you stray from the path. God offers many signs that point to the truth: Scripture, Sacred tradition, Church teaching, the Holy Family and the Saints.

Your mission statement should be clearly displayed in a location all will see. In my home, it is on the refrigerator . . . that important appliance and frequent "gathering" spot for the children (and sadly, myself also). A home altar is another good location.

Your mission statement can also be displayed in other parts of your home—perhaps next to a religious picture, crucifix, or family portrait.

The important thing is to use it regularly. Read it aloud at least weekly within family discussions or family nights or after Sunday mass, and let children participate. Have family discussions about how you have done in the past week. Have you stayed on course? Have you made some gains? Have there been setbacks? How can your family do better next week? How can your family pray about it? Following is a format to try within your family for weekly discussions.

To Stay on Course Weekly

+ Gather together.
+ Open with prayer and Scripture reading.
+ Read your family mission statement aloud.
+ Discuss how your family did in the past week.
+ Encourage suggestions and input for improvements.
+ Reward faithfulness and accomplishment.
+ Close with prayer.

Changing Your Mission Statement

Like recalibrating a navigational instrument, it sometimes may be necessary to make changes in your mission statement. This may be brought about by new insights, changing family roles and activities, or a more refined sense of direction. As your children grow and your family changes, you may need to modify some aspects of your mission statement. This is often the way in which God's Will is revealed. Rather than a once-for-all message, your purpose in life (individual and family) is commonly an "unfolding" process where one layer of God's intent reveals another layer just below it.

As before, have family discussions about the mission statement, past, present, and future, always seeking consensus for a clear and current version. Then write it, use it, and continue referring to it.

Strengthening the Family

There are many resources found in books, magazines, videos, and audiotapes that nourish parents and allow them to feed their children with spiritual insights. Some excellent materials for Catholic parents can be found in the Resource section at the end of this book.

Strong families emerge from parents who are strong in their faith and choose to keep strong by a regular exposure to good Catholic materials, sort of like a diet and exercise program to maintain proper weight, muscle tone, flexibility, and strength. If we routinely go to the fountain and drink, we will continue to bring new life into our family's hearts, minds, and souls (*CCC* 2214).

For Christian men, St. Joseph's Covenant Keepers is an informal, international network under the patronage of St. Joseph, dedicated to strengthening the family by following these eight commitments:

1. Affirming Christ's Lordship Over Our Families
2. Following St. Joseph, the Loving Leader and Head of the Holy Family
3. Loving Our Wives All Our Lives
4. Turning Our Hearts Toward Our Children
5. Educating Our Children in the Discipline and Instruction of the Lord
6. Protecting Our Families
7. Providing for Our Families
8. Building Our Marriages and Families on the "Rock"

These commitments are the basis for growing numbers of men who are serious about their role as husbands and fathers, and the Lordship of Jesus Christ over their families. Stephen Woods' excellent book, *Christian Fatherhood* (Family Life Center Publications, P.O. Box 6060, Pt. Charlotte, FL 33949, 1997), provides a wealth of information about the eight commitments and is must reading for Catholic dads.

Christian women and their femininity have a unique relationship with Mary, Mother of the Redeemer. "Women, by looking to Mary, find in her the secret of living their femininity with dignity and of achieving their own true advancement. In the light of Mary, the church sees in the face of women the reflection of a beauty which mirrors the loftiest sentiments of which the human heart is capable: the self-offering totality of love; the strength that is capable of bearing the greatest sorrows; limitless fidelity and tireless devotion to work; the ability to combine penetrating intuition with words of support and encouragement" (*Mother of the Redeemer*, 46).

Pope John Paul II also offered an Apostolic Letter on "The Dignity and Vocation of Women" (August 15, 1988). Many useful teachings are contained in the document.

I would highly recommend that women also read Johnnette Benkovic's book, *Full of Grace—Women and the Abundant Life* (Servant Publications, P.O. Box 8617, Ann Arbor, Michigan 48107, 1998) which outlines qualities of authentic Catholic womanhood and essential elements for a deeper relationship with God. A number of practical insights are offered, combined with scripture and Church teachings to help women on the path of holiness.

Summary

The Catholic family has the mission (purpose) to become a community of life and love on the earthly pilgrimage to the Father, sharing in the development of society (especially with the poor and disadvantaged) and in the life and mission of the Church. In addition, each family has a unique and personal mission to live a part of God's divine plan for the universe. Discovering God's call for the family becomes vital to staying on course as we journey to eternal life and the ultimate family reunion. A family mission statement visually defines the important qualities and spiritual intention of the family and serves an important role in developing family unity.

✦ ✦ ✦

Holy Family Prayer
(Fr. Larry Toschi, OSJ)

Most Holy Trinity, Father, Son, and Holy Spirit, we adore You. We thank You for Your infinite love in creating us in Your image, becoming incarnate to redeem us, indwelling within our souls. We thank You for the example of the Holy Family in which the Savior of the World was prepared for His mission.

Pour forth Your Spirit upon our family that we may be what You want us to be, a communion of life and love. Let not our individual wants and desires obscure Your wonderful plan for us. Never let hurt or differences or selfishness draw us apart.

Fill us with love and forgiveness toward each other, centered on Your love and forgiveness toward us.

Mary, Mother of the Church, be the mother of our family, a little church.

Joseph, Patron of the Church, guard and protect our family as you guarded and protected Jesus and Mary.

Jesus, Mary, and Joseph, as you always followed the course the Father mapped out for you, so help our family to stay on course toward our eternal destiny with you in the glory of the Most Holy Trinity. Amen.

Family Mission Statement
Work Sheet

1. The virtues that symbolize our family are _____
   _____

2. What phrase or single word describes our family as God
   wants us to be? _____

3. What is most important to our family? _____
   _____

4. What is our family's vision for the future in our
   A. Home _____
   B. Church _____
   C. Society _____

5. What family activities are most important to us?
   A. _____
   B. _____
   C. _____
   D. _____
   E. _____

6. When is the best time for family prayer? _____

7. How can we be a witness to God's love
   A. in our home? _____
   B. in our community? _____

8. In what ways can we serve the poor and disadvantaged?
   _____

9. What scripture passage reflects our family's mission and purpose?
   _____
   _____

10. How can we best deal with problems and difficulties in our family?
    _____
    _____

Family Mission Statement

A Rough Draft

In our family, we will live by the virtues of _____ and

resolve problems by _____

_____.

. . . .

As a community of life and love, we will place great importance

on _____ and share in the life of the

Church by _____

_____.

. . . .

We will place high value on being together as a family, especially

in _____.

We will be a witness to God's love by serving the_____
in our community, and by reflecting the compassion and goodness of
Jesus Christ in our home.

✦ ✦ ✦

I would suggest rewriting the mission statement in your own words
with assistance from other family members. Remember, the mission
statement should not be too long, and should readily encapsulate the
family's purpose as part of God's plan.

Include scripture verses or key words and phrases that quickly illus-
trate what your family is all about.

Chapter 3
The Journey
What We Do Along the Way

There are many practical ways in which your family can follow God's path on your pilgrimage toward His Kingdom. Certainly, the more activities done as a united family, the better—rather than activities that fragment your family and send the members in different directions. A number of suggestions are contained in "The Path" (Chapter 4). Here is a brief summary of what you will find there.

Ways to Stay on Course

Weekly Family Discussions
Weekly Family Nights (or Days)
Family Retreat and Family Fasting
Activities with Other Families
Education in Prayer

Mass and Sharing in the Holy Eucharist
The Holy Rosary for Families
Sacred Heart and Immaculate Heart Consecration
Family Altar
Scripture Reading
Discussing the Lives of the Saints
Home Sacramentals
Teaching Christian Virtues
Storytelling
Catholic Scouting
Fostering Vocations and Life-work Choices

The map guides the traveler, the blueprint guides the builder, and your mission statement guides your family. A Catholic culture within your home becomes daily food for the journey, and keeps you going along the same way that countless other Christian families have walked.

Of course, the only true path is Jesus, whose life can fill your home with unimaginable goodness, love, and forgiveness because He is **THE WAY** and **THE TRUTH**. His map is the only true map. We are led to fullness of life and love because He is also **THE LIFE**.

A Catholic Culture in the Home

Maintaining a Catholic Christian culture within your home allows faith to grow naturally in each individual life. Developing a strong Catholic identity in all members of your family begins with placing Christ at the center of your home just as He was the center of the Holy Family. All relationships between family members and with those outside your home center around Jesus so that difficulties, problems, and positive happenings always have a reference point.

A Catholic culture in your home is simply a way of living, based on your common faith and beliefs. Here are some ways to establish a home life that revolves around being Catholic:

✦ Jesus is at the center of your home.

✦ Jesus is number one in each person's life.

✦ Jesus is first in the Mass, especially in the Real Presence of the Eucharist.

✦ All relationships within your home and those outside your home revolve around Jesus.

✦ Family traditions are an important part of each year.

✦ Family prayer is a daily experience.

✦ Events in the Church calendar (such as Advent and Lent, holy days, saints' feast days) are celebrated at home.

✦ Trusting in God in all circumstances is a common act of faith for everyone in your family, particularly with illness, problems, and struggles.

Growing Together as a Family

Through prayer and an awareness of your Catholic identity, your family grows in:

✦ Love of Jesus
✦ Love of the Church
✦ Love of prayer
✦ Love of the Sacraments
✦ Love of Scripture

✦ Love of Mary, Joseph, the Angels and Saints

✦ Love of being Catholic and of fellow Catholics

✦ Love of all neighbors, especially the poor

Just think how these "loves," steadily increasing in your family, can foster a deep and lasting faith, carrying you and your children along the way to the destination of eternal life with God! Holiness for your family is part of God's divine plan. Whatever degree of holiness that is present within your family occurs through daily contact with the only, true head of households— **God** and the living presence of Christ in each person. Contact with God occurs through family and individual prayer, and with a regular focus toward serving Him. Prayer becomes as normal a daily event as eating.

The True Vine

The Gospel story of the vine and the branches (John 15:1–8) gives a beautiful picture of abiding life in Christ—growing, maturing, and bearing fruit. You are branches attached to the true vine, Jesus, and the Holy Spirit flows into your life, so that you may bear much fruit.

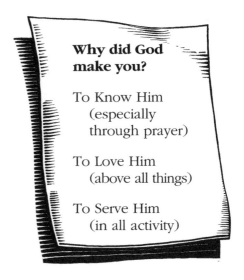

Why did God make you?

To Know Him
(especially through prayer)

To Love Him
(above all things)

To Serve Him
(in all activity)

Children are also attached to parents, and your family is attached to the Church in an abiding presence that reflects God's abundant life and joy.

As members of the Church, you share the common mission of proclaiming the Gospel. This is evangelization, which is the mission of the Church (*The Vocation and Mission of the Lay Faithful in the Church and the World,* 33). This mandate is also recorded in St. Mark's Gospel,

"And he [Christ] said to them, 'Go unto all the world and preach the Gospel to the whole creation.'"
(Mark 16:15)

A Mission for Everyone

Each member of your family has a mission. In **general**, you are witnesses to others of Christ in your life. As Jesus proclaimed in the Great Commission,

"Go therefore and make disciples of all nations, baptizing them in the name of the Father and of the Son and of the Holy Spirit . . ."
(Matthew 28:19)

You can also discover the **specific** way (or ways) God wants you to work for Him, spreading the Gospel message to others. This can be done through example, involvement in your family, Church, and community, and using your abilities to bring glory to God in your actions. These personal lifework choices (personal mission) are part of God's plan for everyone, including single and married people, the young and elderly, and those in the priesthood and religious life.

Discovering your personal mission is a living, dynamic experience, not settled in a single choice. Rather, it is a process that becomes clearer in time and changes as you progress through different stages of life.

Mission and purpose, individually and as a family, can and should be expressed wherever you find yourself—home, school, work, church, or leisure settings. Bloom wherever you are planted!

Our Personal Mission is . . .

To do what God wants
   us to do . . .
to say what God wants
   us to say . . .
to live as God wants us
   to live.

Summary

A home atmosphere that relies on the family's Catholic identity creates a natural place to express faith in God on a daily basis. The family becomes a culture of prayer, devotion, and unity that centers around God and His Son, Jesus Christ. The Church offers so many opportunities for the family to grow in their love of God, especially in the Mass, Sacraments, Scripture, Sacred Tradition, and the Rosary. Parents share in the common evangelical mission of the Church, living and proclaiming the Gospel starting with their children. As God calls the family to a unique mission, so does He call each member of the family to live out their personal way of serving Him.

✦ ✦ ✦

Prayer to the Holy Family
(Pope Leo XIII)

Most Loving Jesus, by your sublime and beautiful virtues and by the example of Your family life you blessed with peace and happiness the family chosen by you on earth. Graciously look on this family humbly kneeling before You and imploring Your mercy. Remember that we belong entirely to You, for it is to You we have in a special way dedicated and devoted ourselves. Look on us in Your loving kindness, preserve us from dangers, and give us the grace to persevere to the end in the imitation of Your Holy Family. After revering and loving You faithfully on earth, may we bless and praise You eternally in heaven.

Mary, our dearest Mother, to your intercession we have recourse, knowing that your divine Son will hear your prayers.

Glorious patriarch, St. Joseph, assist us by your powerful mediation, and offer by the hands of Mary our prayers to Jesus.

Jesus, Mary, and Joseph, enlighten us, assist us, save us. Amen.

Chapter 4
The Path
Practical Ways to Stay on Course

The Holy Family is truly a master work of God's creative power. It was the community where Jesus spent most of His years. You can draw upon the lives of Mary and Joseph as model spouses and parents, and the power of Christ to develop holiness in your own family.

The Holy Family of Nazareth serves as a God-given portrait of family life, and is a source of strength for those Catholic families who want to live their life "in Jesus, through Mary, with Joseph." The vocation and mission of Joseph and Mary can be a fountain of inspiration for the struggles and challenges of raising children.

Pope John Paul II reminds us that "the future of the world and the church passes through the family" (*The Role of the Christian Family in the Modern World*, 75). This powerful statement is often quoted by those who speak about family life and vocations. Indeed, the family serves as rich soil for planting the seeds of vocation, whether one is called to the married life, priesthood, consecrated life, or single life (*CCC* 2222).

Your family can also be a big influence on how children respond to God's call, by encouraging them to listen to His voice in their heart and seek His loving will and guidance in all things through prayer. By developing not just a family mission, but an individual sense of personal mission in each child, young people can begin to recognize their God-given talents, abilities, and gifts, and thus use them in service to God, family, and community.

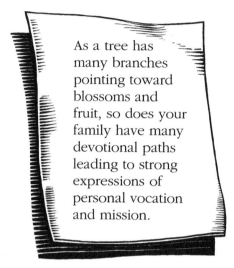

As a tree has many branches pointing toward blossoms and fruit, so does your family have many devotional paths leading to strong expressions of personal vocation and mission.

God has given each family member many gifts. Like any present wrapped in a box and given by someone who loves you, any gift from God must be unwrapped and used. The child who unwraps a present and discovers a ball is not going to leave it in the box. God wants you to use your gifts and use them well.

> *"As each has received a gift, employ it for one another, as good stewards of God's varied grace." (1 Peter 4:10)*

As a tree has many branches pointing toward blossoms and fruit, so does your family have many devotional paths leading to a flowering of faith, hope, and love in your home, resulting in strong expressions of personal vocation and mission. Your family becomes a greenhouse for growing boys and girls into faith-filled adults with God at the very center of their lives.

Family devotions become a way to teach children how to be followers of Jesus. As daily prayer occurs within your home, all members of your family should experience the value of coming together in praise of God and in thanksgiving for His vital presence in living out their vocation and mission.

A number of devotions, family activities, and suggestions for staying on course follow.

Weekly Family Discussions

Having family discussions as a weekly event, such as Sundays after Mass, or during a weeknight, is a great way to teach relationship skills to children and for planning upcoming activities. It is also an opportunity for reviewing the mission statement to see how well your family did in the past week. Besides having a clear sense of purpose and direction through the mission statement, you will likely be concerned with how well the family **communicates** with each other in any situation.

Some of the topics for discussion at weekly family meetings could include:

✦ Our family mission statement—How are we doing?
✦ The life and times of a Saint (chosen by a different family member each week).
✦ A story related to one of the virtues, followed by discussion.
✦ Talents, abilities, and gifts in each family member, with encouragement toward discovery of individual vocations and God's plan in the life of each member.
✦ Planning special family events and activities.

Some of these discussions may require some preparation, especially if younger children are involved. Give strong consideration to establishing a home altar (discussed later in this chapter) as a centerpiece for family discussion.

Weekly Family Nights (or Days)

There is an incredible force waiting to influence your family. Simple in concept, fun in practice, and powerful in nourishing the mind and soul of each family member. It is the scheduled allotment of time on a regular, weekly basis to teach important virtues and matters of faith and experience activities that are fun!

A typical family activity may involve 30–60 minutes of engaging activities and instruction about important beliefs using a variety of resources like board games, videos, storytelling, music, books, or props. For example, a compass and a family treasure hunt (planned in advance) with a map for each child is a great way to have non-stop fun, especially as kids discover the "treasure" (e.g., candy bars) at the end of their search. A family discussion about the compass and the map as metaphors can follow, illustrating how Mary, Joseph, and the Saints always point us toward Christ, who in turn points us to Heaven (as the compass always points north) and how God has a divine plan or "map" for each of us that will lead to our eternal home with Him.

Family nights should be frequent and simple without being highly structured. There must always be room for spontaneity, and a high degree of child involvement. Lectures or long talks from mom or dad stray from the purpose of family nights: to create an exciting, whole-family experience that is enjoyable to all, while teaching important Catholic Christian beliefs.

Don't become too organized, too fancy, too complex in creating the event. Family nights will not necessarily end up as deeply profound religious experiences, but do offer a regular opportunity to reinforce critically important character qualities (virtues) and beliefs.

A variety of activities, changing from week to week, is also a good way to maintain a sense of anticipation and excitement. I would also recommend setting aside the same evening (or day) each week for family time and protecting that time by avoiding distractions like the telephone, TV, or doorbell. This is a special time for family unity and each meeting adds a drop of glue to the bond being formed between family members.

In Deuteronomy 6:5–9 we are told:

". . . and you shall love the Lord your God with all your heart, and with all your soul, and with all your might. And these words which I command you this day shall be upon your heart; and you shall teach them diligently to your children, and shall talk of them when you sit in your house, and when you walk by the way, and when you lie down, and when you rise. And you shall bind them as a sign upon your hand, and they shall be as frontlets between your eyes. And you shall write them on the doorposts of your house and on your gates."

We thus need to jump at the chance to plant seeds in the life of our children, teaching them the essence of our beliefs and giving them the building blocks of strong character virtues.

Creating a family night mentality as parents means that we also discover other opportunities for spontaneous teaching while waiting in line at the supermarket, driving in the car, or cleaning house. Just a simple action like turning off the radio and asking if the broadcaster is still talking can be a simple, effective lesson about prayer. Even when we don't pray, God is still "broadcasting" and we simply need to turn our prayer life to the "on" position. He is always there for us, and He is waiting to come into our homes in a special way during family nights.

Family outings for the evening or the day are also valuable ways for family closeness to develop, just spending time together whether or not a specific activity is planned. For example, the family can go bowling or can just go to a park and be in each other's company without a planned event.

Family Retreat and Family Fasting

In our culture, it is difficult to get away from the many activities and distractions that present themselves daily. Yet our constant exposure to worldly distractions tends to drown out the voice of God and interfere with the Holy Spirit.

A family home retreat is a deliberate effort to turn off the interruptions in our life and spend precious time together as a family, focusing on each other and God in a spirit of common love. Although a family retreat can be a time for silence, it is also a time to be reacquainted with each other through games, stories, prayer, and other creative approaches relevant to the needs of the family.

Of course, a family retreat must begin with eliminating distractions. Turn off the TV, radio,

CD/cassette player, computer, and electronic games. Unplug the phone or let the answering machine take calls. Leave the newspapers by the front door and the mail in the mailbox. Give serious thought to selling electronic products (like television) that offer little more than passive entertainment.

Encourage each family member to look at each other in positive ways. Think about the negative effect of name-calling, sarcasm, put-downs, nagging, whining, and complaining and have discussions about eliminating these responses from daily family life. Compliment each other during the retreat.

Play games. Tell stories from the "good old days." Show family movies and bring out old family photos. Make a video of your family during the retreat and take pictures. Make a poster for each person in the family. Go over your family mission statement and set goals for the future.

Plan you next family vacation. Share the dreams each of you have. Talk about your favorite family memories. Encourage questions about faith and God.

✦ ✦ ✦

Family fasting can occur by giving up things like sweets, television, computer games, or meat on Wednesdays and Fridays. We let our children know that this is an offering to God, and that Wednesday and Friday are the special days we give up something for Christ and His Church.

Certainly, as adults, we can fast by giving up all but bread and water, yet children may need a modified form of fasting according to their age. Adults with certain dietary requirements may also need to modify the way in which they fast.

The beauty of fasting lies in the development of self-sacrifice and self-mastery done in the name of Jesus Christ who gives us the fruits of His own sacrifice.

Activities with Other Families

A family prayer group composed of three to four other families is a wonderful way for children to experience Christian living first-hand. I would particularly recommend a **family Rosary group** where each child leads a decade of the Rosary, along with special prayers and intercessions before or after the Rosary.

Family catechesis is an excellent way to offer instruction in the Catholic faith for both children and adults. The *Faith and Life Series* by Ignatius Press is an outstanding resource for this purpose. This exemplary program can be used for single family religious education in weekly meetings, or with groups of families on a weekly basis in alternating homes. Of course, the *Catechism of the Catholic Church* (*CCC*) is the premier reference for teaching our faith and beliefs as Catholics.

By linking with other families, many opportunities can emerge for doing things together in an atmosphere of common faith. Some examples are:

✦ Camping together.
✦ Celebrating feast days and holidays together.
✦ Having breakfast or lunch after Sunday Mass.
✦ Enjoying "game nights," barbecues, or picnics.

I am especially enthusiastic about family camping. Whether it is just your family, or with other families, there is much value in camping outdoors. It provides an opportunity to work and play together, talk together, and create memories that will linger for years and years. Family camping removes the distractions of society, and places you in the center of God's miraculous creation. You feel small, and visually experience all the natural wonders of the universe. From my own experience as a father of five children, the flashlights, tents, sleeping bags, campfires, star-filled sky, and crisp mountain air have strong appeal for children.

Education in Prayer

Prayer is essential for life. It is not something simply "added on" to life. Done regularly, prayer becomes as habitual an activity as other parts of life, like eating or breathing (*CCC* 2685).

Family prayer is prayer offered in communion—husband with wife, parents with children (*The Role of the Christian Family in the Modern World*, 59). As Catholic parents, you also have the responsibility for teaching your children to pray through a personal dialogue with God (*The Role of the Christian Family in the Modern World*, 60). The home and Church become classrooms of prayer where your children learn about:

✦ Traditional Catholic prayers (like the Hail Mary, Glory Be, Our Father)

✦ Sacraments (such as Confession, Holy Communion, Confirmation)

✦ The Mass

✦ The Rosary

✦ Prayer for special intentions (such as for specific friends or family members, vocations to the priesthood and religious life)

✦ The Saints and how they prayed

By teaching your children to pray, read the Bible, and see how God has been revealed throughout creation, you then nourish the faith of your children, so they can bear good fruit. In the lesson offered by Christ, St. Matthew states:

> *"So, every sound tree bears good fruit, but the bad tree bears evil fruit. A sound tree cannot bear evil fruit, nor can a bad tree bear good fruit." (Matthew 7:17–18)*

Choose a specific time each day or evening for family prayer. (See Fr. Michael Scanlan's book, *Appointment with God.*)

Mass and Sharing in the Holy Eucharist

The Holy Eucharist is at the very source of Christian life and marriage (*The Role of the Christian Family in the Modern World*, 57).

When your Catholic family shares in the Eucharistic meal, the individual members truly become one body, linking themselves with the greater body of the Church (*CCC* 2181).

Your small "family church" is united with other families, proclaiming a common identity of life and love in the big, extended family of God. Heaven becomes the ultimate family vacation. Each time you worship at Mass and share in the Eucharist, you step into God's kingdom for a little while. You are united with centuries of other families in Heaven in their eternal praise of God.

Teaching your children special love for the Holy Eucharist and the real presence of Christ is one of the greatest gifts that can be given to them. Adoration and love of Christ's Eucharistic presence provides many graces and strength for your family (*CCC* 1418). See the Resource section for materials on Eucharistic adoration

The Eucharist "*is for you, dear husbands and wives, parents and families!* Did Jesus not institute the Eucharist in a family-like setting during the Last Supper? When you meet for meals and are together in harmony, *Christ*

is close to you. And he is Emmanuel, God with us, in an even greater way whenever you approach the table of the Eucharist" (*Letter to Families*, 19).

The Holy Rosary for Families

Pope John Paul II, on numerous occasions, has referred to the Rosary as a powerful prayer for this age. Pope Paul VI strongly recommended the recitation of the family Rosary, describing the Rosary as one of the best prayers in common that the Christian family can offer (*Apostolic Exhortation for the Right Ordering and Development of Devotion to the Blessed Virgin Mary*, 1974).

Try praying one decade of the Rosary each evening, having a different child or adult lead the prayers. A special intention, chosen by the leader, can be offered for the decade.

As an alternative, each child can pray a portion of the decade, depending upon the number of children involved. For example, if there are three children and two parents praying the Rosary, each can offer two "Hail Mary's" during the decade.

Of course, a complete, five decade Rosary would also be a wonderful family devotion, but this often depends on the age of the children that participate. The prayers and mysteries of the Marian Rosary, St. Joseph Rosary, and Holy Family Rosary are found on pages 65–70.

Sacred Heart and Immaculate Heart Consecration

Consecration to the Sacred Heart of Jesus is a devotion to the profound, burning, passionate love that the Son of God has for us. A home enthronement is a special ceremony where an image of the Sacred Heart of Jesus is "enthroned" in a prominent location within your home and your family is consecrated to Him.

An outline for this ceremony, pictures, and Sacred Heart prayers are available from the *National Enthronement Center* (see "Resources" section). They also offer a video showing an enthronement ceremony within a Catholic home.

The following "Prayer to the Sacred Heart" can be offered daily by your family:

Prayer to the Sacred Heart
(Priests of the Sacred Heart)

Most Loving Heart of Jesus Fountain of every blessing, I adore You and love You. With deep sorrow for my sins I offer You my heart. Make me humble, patient, pure And totally obedient to Your Will. Grant, good Jesus, That I may live in You And for You. Protect me in the midst of danger, Comfort me in my afflictions. Give me health of body, Assistance in my needs, Your blessing on all that I do And the grace of a holy death. Amen.

Similarly, consecration to the Immaculate Heart of Mary entrusts the family to the love and protection of the Blessed Mother. Like St. Joseph, she provides help in living out our baptismal vows. An image of the Immaculate Heart in every bedroom of the home can be a strong, daily reminder of Mary's care and guidance.

Family Consecration to the Immaculate Heart of Mary
(Christopher Knuffke, OCDS)

O Blessed Virgin Mary, we place ourselves before your image as a family, we consecrate ourselves to your Immaculate Heart.

To you we entrust our sorrows, cares, and joys in all the circumstances of our lives.

O Mother of God and our mother, watch over our family this day, and every day. Help us become a holy family, in imitation of the Holy Family.

In all our work and play, direct us Holy Mother to your Son, Jesus Christ. May He always be the center of our family life.

When this earthly life comes to an end, may our family be reunited in Heaven with Jesus, Mary and Joseph. Immaculate Heart of Mary, pray for us! Amen.

Family Altar

The family altar can be a simple bookshelf, table, or mantle with a combination of elements that image our Catholic identity, like

+ Religious Art
+ Crucifix
+ Holy Water
+ Candles
+ Holy Bible
+ Statues

The physical location should be a prominent place where the altar can be seen by anyone coming into your home, and where family prayer takes place.

Our family altar consists of a picture of the Sacred Heart of Jesus and of the Immaculate Heart of Mary, a 7-day blessed church-type candle in a glass container, a bible, and a plant. If religious art is used, the likely choices will reflect the devotion of your family to a particular Saint or member of the Holy Family.

Creating a family altar is a visible expression of your faith and identity as a Catholic family, recognized by more than children and family visitors, but also by neighbors, friends, acquaintances, and workers. More than once, a plumber or painter has commented on our altar and good discussions have occurred about our beliefs as Catholics.

Of particular value is the candle. When lit during evening prayer (such as a Rosary decade and Sacred Heart prayer, followed by special intentions), it becomes a central focus to minimize distractions.

Scripture Reading

The written Word of God can speak to families in very powerful ways. Your family should place a special emphasis on Bible reading as Divine Revelation of God's presence in the lives of others, and as a means for your family to grow in knowledge of Him. Sacred Scripture is an integral part of liturgical worship in Mass, and the readings can be discussed among family members daily or on Sunday.

Family Bible reading can be accomplished easily. General Scripture selections can be read aloud by one or more family members daily or weekly, followed by discussion in applying passages to daily life. The Holy Bible (Revised Standard Version) published by Ignatius Press is excellent.

There are also numerous books, commentaries and Bible study programs to facilitate better understanding of scripture, most of which are written at the adult level. For young children, Bible "story" books are an excellent introduction to Scripture and the people in God's family.

Consider a Bible enthronement in your home, placing the Holy Bible in a permanent place for your family's regular use. Perhaps a crucifix, religious art, flowers, candles, or holy water font can be arranged around the Bible. The Bible enthronement can also be part of your family home altar.

Discussing the Lives of Saints

Saints are extended members of the Christian family and role models for us today. They are also terrific examples of how God has chosen **very ordinary people** to reflect His presence in this world.

Saints are the work of Christ, akin to Da Vinci's paintings or Bach's concertos. Through their works, we learn about these artists. It is through the Saints that we learn about God.

Learning about the Saints can occur daily, weekly, or on special feast days that recognize a particular Saint. A special effort can be made by parents to encourage a good understanding of those Saints bearing the name of family members.

Resource materials abound for family activities related to Saints, including *Holy Traders* cards showing various Saints. These laminated cards are similar in appearance to sports-type trading cards, and offer graphics and text well-suited to youth. They are available in sets of 40.

The Saints Kit is a collection of 189 large Saint cards featuring inspirational stories. All the Saints of the Roman calendar and more are included. Each card has information about the Saint's life, feast day, dates of birth and death, year of canonization, and picture. The cards are suitable for grades 4 through adult. Refer to the "Resources" section at the end of this book for various materials on Saints.

Home Sacramentals

Sacramentals are sacred signs instituted by the Church that prepare us to receive God's grace. Among them, *blessings* are of primary importance (*CCC* 1617 and 1677).

Providing a blessing to each of your children is another way to remind them of who they are as God's created work. Since they are formed in the image and likeness of God, blessing your children each day is a sign of daily membership in the body of Christ and true identity as believers.

A blessing can be done simply by making the sign of the cross on the forehead of each child at the beginning and end of each day, and by having holy water present in the home so that parents and children can bless themselves at the beginning and/or end of the day. The holy water can be contained in a small font located near a frequently used

doorway, or can be in each bedroom of the home.

Evening prayers can also conclude with parents blessing children while tracing the Sign of the Cross on their forehead.

Wearing the brown Scapular of Our Lady of Mount Carmel is a sign of love for Mary and of consecration to her Immaculate Heart. It is easily introduced in the home. In fact, wearing the scapular is a wonderful complement to the Rosary.

The word "scapular" is from the Latin "scapulae" meaning shoulders. The Scapular is a sacramental that represents a small form of the Carmelite religious habit, consisting of two pieces of cloth connected by a ribbon-like material, worn so that one piece hangs in front and the other in back. It symbolizes devotion to Mary. The Scapular is typically worn under one's clothing. (See the "Resources" section at the end of this book for information on ordering Scapulars.)

Other sacramentals that are important expressions of our faith and Catholic identity include medals, crucifixes, sacred images (i.e., art and statues), holy oils, relics, incense, ashes, palms, candles and the Rosary. The use of sacramentals enhance the Catholic culture in the family, and prepares souls to receive whatever grace God wishes to provide.

Teaching Christian Virtues

The lighthouse that shines its piercing beam through foul weather lets the approaching ship know where to sail. Even though the ship's crew has charts and maps that help them find their way, storms can throw a ship off course toward potential disaster. So, too, can the temptations of life throw you off course.

Christian virtues are the lighthouse, shining a powerful beacon on your path to guide you through the journey of life by establishing a standard. Christian virtues are a witness to the presence of Jesus Christ in your life, particularly as Godly examples for your children.

Children see you as you are, **not** as you would like them to see you.

Christian virtues are firm attitudes and perfections of the mind and will acquired by God's grace.

Developing Christian virtues in your children (and yourselves for that matter) is no small task, since virtues are such brilliant qualities of moral excellence. Christian virtues represent the highest good that can be accomplished according to Christian standards and, once present, become a habit of choosing excellence in behavior and conduct. The family that emphasizes the importance of virtues builds a foundation on goodness (*CCC* 1810).

As parents, you offer powerful modeling effects for virtue formation in your children, especially by example, word, and practice (*CCC* 2223).

Example—What is **witnessed** in the home from parents' actions.

Word—What is **told,** particularly by family discussions and storytelling.

Practice—What is **done** by parents and children at home, school, work, church, and community.

Some of the virtues that can be taught in the family are:

✦ Faith (belief in God and all that He has said and revealed; unites with works to be truly alive; *CCC* 1842)

✦ Hope (belief in God's promises and mercy; relying on the promises of Jesus and grace from the Holy Spirit; *CCC* 1843)

✦ Charity (loving God above all things and loving your neighbor as yourself; *CCC* 1844; John 13:34)

✦ Prudence (wisdom, insight, understanding; *CCC* 1835)

✦ Justice (fairness; *CCC* 1836)

✦ Fortitude (boldness, bravery; *CCC* 1837)

✦ Temperance (restraint, strength of character; *CCC* 1838)

✦ Compassion (deep concern)

✦ Loyalty (faithfulness)

✦ Honesty (truth)

✦ Work (applying one's self, commitment)

✦ Friendship (companionship)

✦ Courtesy (accommodation, favor)

✦ Kindness (generosity, helpfulness)

The four virtues—prudence, justice, fortitude, temperance are known as the "cardinal" virtues, and come from the Latin word for hinge, since all the other virtues, lesser and greater in their importance, pivot or hinge on these four specific virtues. They are next in importance to the "theological" virtues ("theological" because they come from God) of faith, hope, and charity.

The foundation for Christian moral activity takes root in the theological virtues of faith, hope, and charity.

Virtues are all gifts from God and rely on Christ as the norm. We must remember as parents that self-mastery is an ongoing process that requires renewed effort at different times in our life (*CCC* 2342).

Story Telling

Story telling and story reading are two of the best ways to convey important, timeless virtues to your children, and stay on the right track. Some of the best lessons about faith can be taught by real-life anecdotes and events—especially those that you have experienced as parents and which you observe in your family. Children also love to hear stories about themselves when they were younger, events perhaps that they no longer recall, but can be retold by parents.

They also enjoy stories about cousins, uncles and aunts, grandparents, and other extended family members that reflect the human experience. While often humorous, these stories can also be a rich source of passing on what you value as important ways of responding to circumstances in life.

Story telling should not be limited to the past, but also should include present, day-to-day ups and downs, and your response to the events at work, school, and home.

Tell stories as often as possible; Jesus did. The gospels are filled with parables and stories offered from God's Son and they were recounted for what was undoubtedly a powerful impact on the listeners of His time. These stories continue to have impact on us today as they have over the centuries.

Tell a story at the dinner table, while driving in the car with the kids, when making breakfast, and at bedtime. Children especially enjoy being characters in fictitious stories.

Special stories on the important virtues in life can be found in a number of excellent books that can be read aloud in a family gathering. Older children will want to participate in the reading. Let them! Include your children as much as possible in reading and telling stories, and be sure to discuss the meaning of the story when it is over.

Catholic Scouting

Scouting represents an outstanding approach for youth ministry. The Boy Scouts of America, in cooperation with the Catholic Church, offers a proven and highly effective program that prepares boys for a life of service, leadership and giving. The Girl Scouts have a similar program.

Adult spiritual development is also an important element of scouting; adult leaders, called Scouters, work closely with those in cub packs or scout troops and can have a very positive influence on their spiritual formation.

The implications for your family are obvious. Families that become involved with their children in scouting programs can develop particularly close bonds when doing scout activities together. In addition, the Boy Scouts of America promotes a special family program centered on family talks on a number of subjects including sharing, caring, trusting, giving, communicating, developing talents, and developing family roots and traditions.

Scouting fosters the development of ideals related to God, family, and the community. In addition, boys and girls have special programs for religious emblems and awards related to their Catholic Faith.

Some of the typical benefits common to the Catholic scouting experience are:

◆ Scouting within the parish allows friendships and spiritual bonds to develop among youth, and also among adult leaders.
◆ Scouting provides youth with adult role models, dedicated to their faith and their church community.
◆ Scouting encourages participation in parish life, including regular Mass attendance and helping with church functions. Scouting provides opportunities for spiritual growth and development, especially through the Religious Emblems Program and special outings.

The scouting program is designed so that one can enter at any level, based on grade and age. The Cub Scout program is for boys in grades 1 to 5, and the Boy Scout program is for those in grades 6 to 12. Explorer Scouts (boys and girls) participate from grades 9 to college. In Girl Scouts, the program is open to girls ages 5 to 17.

Fostering Vocations and Lifework Choices

Pope John Paul II in his *Letter to Families* states:

"Parents are the first and most important educators of their own children and they also possess a fundamental competence in this area: they are educators because they are parents. . . . Within the context of education, due attention must be paid to the essential question of *choosing a vocation*, and here in particular that of *preparing for marriage*" (*Letters to Families*, 16)

Parents can and should play a vital role in fostering vocations within the home, beginning with an understanding of the universal vocation we have from baptism to grow in holiness. Each family member needs to discover the unique, personal vocation God has designed for them (*CCC* 1877 and 2223).

Remember the Gospel story of the rich young man (See Mark 10:17–22.)? He asked Jesus, "What must I do to inherit eternal life?" The Pope teaches that he was really asking:

"What must I do so that my life may have meaning?"

"What is God's plan for my life?"

"What is His will?"

These questions are similar to others asked by youth, like:

"What is my purpose in life?"

"What am I doing here, anyway?"

"Where am I going?"

To help your children answer these questions, teach them that God calls each person to a very special plan (vocation and mission). You can help by showing the importance of finding and responding to the personal vocation that God wants to reveal. Everyone has a special place in God's plan, using the talents, abilities and gifts that He has furnished.

Fostering vocations to the priesthood and consecrated life often comes about by just reinforcing the need to listen for God's call in a spirit of prayer, and being aware of external circumstances in daily life. You can also promote an awareness that skills are truly gifts from the Creator, and that each child is called according to God's plan and purpose.

God's Call within the Family

There are many ways to encourage an awareness of God's call within your family. Here are some suggestions:

✦ Talk with your children about what priests, religious brothers or sisters have meant in your life.

✦ Encourage faithful Mass attendance, including Holy Days and special feast days.

✦ Invite priests and others in the religious life into your home for meals or family events.

✦ Offer examples from Scripture of God's call, such as the story of Mary and Joseph, Peter, Martha and Mary, Abram and Sarai, Jeremiah.

✦ Share stories about the Saints that reflect their response to God's call using books, videos, and other material.

- ✦ Make a pilgrimage to a Shrine or visit a neighboring parish.
- ✦ Get involved in your parish.
- ✦ Take your children to Confession regularly, and use these times as opportunities to pray.
- ✦ Encourage great love and adoration of Jesus' real Presence in the Eucharist.
- ✦ Pray the family Rosary on a regular basis, allowing your children to lead different decades.
- ✦ Offer daily prayers for an awareness of God's plan for each child, and also pray for vocations to the priesthood and religious life.
- ✦ Have your children involved as much as possible in parish life, such as altar service, scouting, and the Junior Legion of Mary.

Above all, be open to however God may be calling your child. Do not attempt to sell, persuade, or discourage them on a particular choice. Pray for them.

Also realize that God may not come calling directly into the hearts of your children, but may bring His message through the circumstances of life, friends, and other family members. Thus, God's call may be discovered internally or externally.

As parents, you must also be mindful of your own personal vocation and continually remain open to how God might lead you. A decision to marry, for example, is a commitment which entails a subsequent spiritual unfolding, from the initial Sacramental vow to a lifetime of additional commitments.

In fostering vocations within the home, you have a unique opportunity to provide lessons in love and faith as your children grow. God chose a family as the vehicle for bringing His Son into the world. It is through your family that children can find their vocation and state of life, and the various gifts that God provides so that they can be sent forth to serve Him and bring glory to His name. You are indispensable in the process of helping your children identify and use their unique gifts in following their vocation as part of God's family, *"for the gifts and the call of God are irrevocable"* (*Romans 11:29*).

In order to receive the call, we must first listen for it. Teaching your children to look and listen for God in their lives is one of the **most important roles** you play as parent, teacher, guide, and mentor of your children's spiritual development.

Refer to the LifeWork book and video noted in the Resource section. These materials focus squarely on the issue of God's call and discovering a true sense of purpose in life.

Summary

There are many tools and weapons that the family can rely upon to defend against worldly influences and Satan's effort to destroy family life. Choosing and using a variety of devotional practices and unity-building activities will do much to strengthen the Catholic identity adopted by parents and children alike. A special emphasis should be placed on fostering an understanding of God's call to a personal vocation and mission, with parents actively involved in guiding their children towards solid, faith-filled lifework choices.

✦ ✦ ✦

Family Prayer

Lord, we belong to You.
We are your family.
Bless us with love for each other.
Bless us with peace and joy.
Bless us with grace to be like Jesus, Mary, and Joseph.
Help us look for the positive in each other.
Help us forgive each other.
Jesus, Son of God,
You are at the center of our family.
Guide us as we work together,
Grow in faith and share Your love in
our home and with others.
We ask this in Your Name. Amen.

✦ ✦ ✦

Chapter 5
The Destination
God's Kingdom

Your purpose for living in this world, for traveling on life's journey is, in a single word, your **destiny**—to love and to eventually live with God forever in His eternal Kingdom. You were created out of love and for love.

By following God's personal plan for your family, you stay on track. You are the train, Jesus is the track, and Heaven is the last stop. Without a clear statement of your mission as a family, the train is more likely to stall, crash, or get switched onto tracks leading in the wrong direction. The enemy (Satan) delights when this occurs. Your true identity, both individually and as a family, becomes muddled if you listen to the world rather than God

and if you do not understand what God wants for your family. Like trains, you are either on the track or off the track (*CCC* 2207).

Building Blocks

The Church accompanies your Christian family on its journey **through** life and **to** life on the "earthly pilgrimage toward God's Kingdom" (*The Role of the Christian Family in the Modern World*, 65).

You are building blocks for establishing this Kingdom by active involvement in the life and mission of the Church (*The Role of the Christian Family in the Modern World*, 49). There are many ways in which the Christian family is profoundly connected to the church, so that you become a "church in miniature" or the "domestic church."

The Christian family is supported by the Church in a number of ways:

✦ By proclaiming the Word of God, the Church reveals to the Christian family its true **identity:** what it is and should be according to God's plan.

✦ By celebrating the Sacraments, the Church enriches and strengthens the Christian family with the grace of Christ, for its sanctification to the glory of the Father.

✦ By the continuous proclamation of Christ's new commandment of love, the Church guides and encourages the Christian family to the service of love, so that it may imitate and relive the same self-giving and sacrificial love that the Lord Jesus had for the entire human race. (*The Role of the Christian Family in the Modern World*, 49)

The Christian family not only **receives** Christ's love, but is called upon to **convey** this love to those in the community.

Pope John Paul II teaches that the family is where the duty to society begins (*The Vocation and Mission of the Lay Faithful in the Church and the World*, 40). He describes the family as "a cradle of life and love," the place in which the individual "is born" or "grown." The family is the basic cell of society. The family is to society what the cell is to a living organism—the basic building block.

Who—or What—Comes First?

Jesus is King of Kings and wants to be King of your home. Can you invite Him into your home as King?

He will make your home a holy place and those within it a holy family. As Jesus was the center of the Holy Family of Nazareth, you can also make Him the center of your home and of the individual lives dwelling within. He is first in the life of believing families. He is the ultimate priority, vastly more important than the distractions of TV, sports, computer games, success and wealth building, music, recreation, materialism, or hobbies.

"Dear brothers and sisters, spouses and parents, this is how the bridegroom *is with you*. You know that he is the Good Shepherd. You know who he is, and you know his voice. You know where he is leading you, and how he strives to give you pastures where you can find life and find it in abundance. You know how he withstands the marauding wolves, and is ever ready to rescue his sheep: every husband and wife, every son and daughter, every member of your families" (*Letter to Families*, 69)

The Holy Family—Jesus, Mary, and Joseph—is the model for all families of all ages. Join them in offering to God the family that you are becoming—a community of life, love, and hope, doing what God wants you to do.

Through discovery of true family purpose, defined in the mission statement, you will understand the process of getting to your destination. The way will be clearly seen, and by living out your family mission in the home, society, and Church, you will make steady progress to heaven and the ultimate family reunion!

Summary

It is vital that the family maintain an eternal perspective, even in the day-to-day events that unfold. Sometimes there are issues within the home that appear as obstacles to unity, yet grace is abundantly available so that parents will be well-equipped to handle the broad range of events that can occur, from tragedy to triumph and from setbacks to victories. Like St. Paul (Phil. 3:14), God wants us to win the prize at the end of the race. He wants us to come home and be part of the eternal chorus of angels, saints, and other families in Heaven.

✦ ✦ ✦

Jesus, King of Kings and King of families, guide our family in all that we do.
We place You in the center of our hearts and home.

Mary, Mother of Jesus and Queen of Families, give us your motherly protection and counsel.

Joseph, Guardian of Jesus and protector of families, serve as an example of holiness in the daily events of family life.

May the Holy Spirit guide our family in all our thoughts, words, and deeds. May God the Father give us the grace to grow as a community of life, love, and hope through Christ our Lord. Amen.

✦ ✦ ✦

Conclusion

The family is, in each instance, a unique, unrepeatable work of creation. At its very heart is the profound, passionate love of God. Each member of the family becomes an essential part of God's divine plan for the universe and, in particular, the message of the Gospel.

Parents have been entrusted with the amazing responsibility of raising children made in the image and likeness of God. **He will provide all the tools and grace necessary to accomplish this purpose.** We can trust Him to do this because we know God has a special love for families. He has already given us a portrait of true family unity in the Holy Family. In the mystery of salvation, God sent His Son into the heart of a family. Joseph and Mary are timeless teachers for authentic parenthood, especially in their abandonment to divine will and dedicated service to Jesus.

We must always trust that God will help us become a family of life, love, unity, and peace. He would never give us children only to ignore our need for special help when it comes to raising them properly. We must ask for His divine intervention at every step of the way in our efforts to raise good children and we must pray with confidence that He knows all of our needs. Grace is operative, thanks be to God!

The family is the perfect place to also foster a genuine sense of personal vocation and mission. Parents and children alike can discover true meaning and purpose in life: becoming who God wants them to be and doing what God wants them to do.

By following Christ, and placing Him in a Kingship position within our home, we will stay on course towards an eternal encounter with the God of the universe, Joseph and Mary, all the angels and saints, and centuries of families who have gone before us.

Praise be to Jesus Christ, now and forever.
Mary, Queen of Families, pray for us.
Joseph, Protector of Families, pray for us.

References

Apostolic Exhortation for the Right Ordering and Development of Devotion to the Blessed Virgin Mary—Marialis Cultos. Pope Paul VI, Pauline Books and Media, Boston, Massachusetts, February 2, 1974.

Catechism of the Catholic Church. English translation of the *Catechism of the Catholic Church* for the United States of America, 1994, United States Catholic Conference, Inc., Libreria Editrice Vaticana.

Christian Fatherhood. Stephen Wood, Family Life Center Publications, Pt. Charlotte, Florida, 1997.

Guardian of the Redeemer: On the Person and Mission of St. Joseph in the Life of Christ and of the Church—Redemptoris Custos. Pope John Paul II, Pauline Books and Media, Boston, Massachusetts, August 15, 1989.

Ignatius Bible. The Revised Standard Version—Catholic Edition. Ignatius Press.

Letter to Families. Pope John Paul II, Pauline Books and Media, Boston, Massachusetts, February 2, 1994.

Mother of the Redeemer (Redemptoris Mater) On the Blessed Virgin Mary in the Life of the Pilgrim Church. Pope John Paul II, Pauline Books and Media, Boston, Massachusetts, March 25, 1987.

The Role of the Christian Family in the Modern World—Familiaris Consortio. Pope John Paul II, Pauline Books and Media, Boston, Massachusetts, November 22, 1981.

The Vocation and Mission of the Lay Faithful in the Church and in the World—Christifideles Laici. Pope John Paul II, Pauline Books and Media, Boston, Massachusetts, December 30, 1988.

The Rosary
To Jesus through Mary

The Rosary draws your family to contemplate the mysteries of salvation. It can easily be part of your daily prayer life, and can be offered in solitude or with a group. The family Rosary is a very special way of coming together in prayer and unity.

Through the centuries, there has always been a special devotion to the Blessed Virgin Mary, the Mother of God. The custom of the Church is to pray five decades of the Rosary per day. During the recitation of each decade, we are given a mystery to meditate upon. The Holy Rosary is usually prayed with beads to denote each Hail Mary and Our Father.

How to Pray the Rosary

1. Make the Sign of the Cross.
2. Say the Apostle's Creed.
3. Say the Our Father.
4. Say three Hail Mary's.
5. Say the Glory Be to the Father
6. Announce the First Mystery.
7. Say the Our Father.
8. Say ten Hail Mary's.
9. Say the Glory Be to the Father
10. Say the Fatima Decade Prayer.
11. Announce the Second Mystery, then say the Our Father, 10 Hail Mary's, Glory Be to the Father, and the Fatima Decade Prayer.
12. Announce the Third Mystery, then say the Our Father, 10 Hail Mary's, Glory Be to the Father, and the Fatima Decade Prayer.
13. Announce the Fourth Mystery, then say the Our Father, 10 Hail Mary's, Glory Be to the Father, and the Fatima Decade Prayer.
14. Announce the Fifth Mystery, then say the Our Father, 10 Hail Mary's, Glory Be to the Father, and the Fatima Decade Prayer.
15. After the Fifth Mystery, say the Hail Holy Queen.
16. Conclude by saying the Last Prayer of the Rosary and make the Sign of the Cross.

Prayers of the Rosary

The Sign of the Cross

In the name of the Father, and of the Son, and of the Holy Spirit. Amen.

The Apostle's Creed

I believe in God, the Father almighty, creator of heaven and earth,
I believe in Jesus Christ his only Son, our Lord.
He was conceived by the power of the Holy Spirit and born of the
    Virgin Mary.
He suffered under Pontius Pilate, was crucified, died, and was buried.
He descended to the dead.
On the third day He rose again.
He ascended into Heaven, and is seated at the right hand of the Father.
He will come again to judge the living and the dead.
I believe in the Holy Spirit,
    the holy Catholic Church,
    the Communion of Saints,
    the forgiveness of sins,
    the resurrection of the body
    and the life everlasting. Amen.

Our Father

Our Father, who art in heaven, hallowed be Thy name. Thy kingdom come, Thy will be done on earth as it is in heaven. Give us this day our daily bread, and forgive us our trespasses as we forgive those who trespass against us, and lead us not into temptation, but deliver us from evil. Amen.

Hail Mary

Hail Mary, full of grace; the Lord is with you; blessed are you among women, and blessed is the fruit of your womb, Jesus. Holy Mary, Mother of God, pray for us sinners, now and at the hour of our death. Amen.

Glory Be to the Father

Glory be to the Father, and to the Son, and to the Holy Spirit. As it was in the beginning, is now, and ever shall be, world without end. Amen.

The Fatima Decade Prayer

O my Jesus, forgive us our sins, save us from the fires of Hell. Lead all souls to Heaven, especially those most in need of Thy mercy. Amen.

Hail, Holy Queen

(Salve Regina)

Hail, holy Queen, Mother of Mercy. Our life, our sweetness, and our hope. To thee do we cry, poor banished children of Eve; to thee do we send up our sighs, mourning and weeping in this valley of tears. Turn then, most gracious Advocate, thine eyes of mercy toward us, and after this our exile, show unto us the blessed fruit of thy womb, Jesus. O clement, O loving, O sweet Virgin Mary.

Pray for us, O holy Mother of God, that we may be made worthy of the promises of Christ. Amen.

Last Prayer of the Rosary

O God, whose only begotten Son, by His life, death, and resurrection, has purchased for us the rewards of eternal life, grant, we beseech thee, that meditating on these mysteries of the most Holy Rosary of the Blessed Virgin Mary, we may imitate what they contain, and obtain what they promise. Through the same Christ our Lord. Amen.

Prayer of Pope Leo XIII to St. Joseph after the Rosary

To you, O Blessed Joseph, we come in our trials, and having asked the help of your most holy spouse, we confidently ask your patronage also. Through that sacred bond of charity which united you to the Immaculate Virgin Mother of God and through the fatherly love with which you embraced the Child Jesus, we humbly beg you to look graciously upon the beloved inheritance which Jesus Christ purchased by his blood, and to aid us in our necessities with your power and strength.

O most provident guardian of the Holy Family, defend the chosen children of Jesus Christ. Most beloved father, dispel the evil of falsehood and sin. Our most mighty protector, graciously assist us from heaven in our struggle with the powers of darkness. And just as you once saved the Child Jesus from mortal danger, so now defend God's Holy Church from the snares of her enemies and from all adversity. Shield each one of us by your constant protection, so that, supported by your example and your help, we may be able to live a virtuous life, to die a holy death, and to obtain eternal happiness in heaven. Amen.

Mysteries of the Marian Rosary

JOYFUL MYSTERIES

*Said on Mondays and Thursdays, and on the Sundays from
the First Sunday of Advent until Lent.*

1. Annunciation of the birth of Jesus to Mary (*Luke 1:26–38*).
2. Visitation of Mary to her cousin Elizabeth (*Luke 1:39–47*).
3. Nativity of Jesus Christ (*Luke 2:1–7*).
4. Presentation of the infant Jesus in the Temple (*Luke 2:22–32*).
5. Finding of the Child Jesus in the Temple (*Luke 2:1–52*).

SORROWFUL MYSTERIES

Said on Tuesdays and Fridays, and the Sundays for Lent

1. Agony of Christ in the Garden (*Mark 14:32–36*).
2. Scourging at the Pillar (*John 18:28–38; 19:1*).
3. Crowning with thorns (*Mark 15:16–20*).
4. Carrying the Cross (*John 19:12–16*).
5. Crucifixion of our Lord Jesus Christ (*Luke 23:33–34; 39–46*).

GLORIOUS MYSTERIES

Said on Wednesdays and Saturdays, and the Sundays from Easter until Advent

1. Resurrection of our Lord from the dead (*Luke 24:1–6a*).
2. Ascension of our Lord into Heaven (*Luke 24:50–53*).
3. Descent of the Holy Spirit upon the apostles on Pentecost (*Acts 2:1–4*).
4. Assumption of the Blessed Virgin Mary into Heaven (*Song of Songs 2:8–14*).
5. Coronation of the Virgin Mary (*Revelation 12:1–6*).

Mysteries of the St. Joseph Rosary

(from the Oblates of St. Joseph)

May be prayed just as Marian Rosary, substituting "Hail Mary" with the following:

Joseph, son of David, and husband of Mary, we honor you, guardian of the Redeemer, and we adore the child you named Jesus.

St. Joseph, patron of the universal church, pray with us, that we may imitate you in lifelong dedication to the interests of the Savior. Amen.

All other prayers of the Rosary, including opening and closing prayers, remain the same.

1. Betrothal to Mary (*Matthew 1:18*).
2. Annunciation to Joseph (*Matthew 1:19–21*).
3. Birth and Naming of Jesus (*Matthew 1:22–25*).
4. Flight into Egypt (*Matthew 2:13–15*).
5. Hidden Life at Nazareth (*Matthew 2:23; Luke 2:51–52*).

Mysteries of the Holy Family Rosary

(from the Oblates of St. Joseph)

May be prayed as the Marian Rosary, substituting the following prayer for the "Hail Mary":

Mary, full of grace, and Joseph, son of David; honor to you, Mother of God, and to you, guardian of the Redeemer. Eternal praise to the child with whom you formed a family, Jesus.

Holy spouses, pray for us sinners, our families and communities, now and at the hour of our death. Amen.

All other prayers of the Rosary, including opening and closing prayers, remain the same.

MYSTERIES

1. Betrothal of Mary and Joseph (*Matthew 1:18, Luke 1:26–27, 2:4–5*).
2. Annunciation to Mary (*Luke 1:28–38*).
3. Annunciation to Joseph (*Matthew 1:19–23*).
4. Joseph takes Mary as his wife (*Matthew 1:24–25*).
5. Birth of Jesus (*Luke 2:6, 15–16*).
6. Circumcision of Jesus (*Luke 2:21*).
7. Presentation of Jesus (*Luke 2:22–40*).
8. Escape into Egypt (*Matthew 2:13–15*).
9. Finding of Jesus in the Temple (*Luke 2:41–50*).
10. Hidden Life at Nazareth (*Luke 2:51–52*).

Resources

There is a wealth of good family books and resources to help you with the task of staying on course. These materials can be of great benefit to your family as a way of gathering ideas for use in your home, for having lively family gatherings, and building better bridges of communication among family members.

Chapter 1—The Holy Family

Apostolic Exhortation for the Right Ordering and Development of Devotion to the Blessed Virgin Mary—Marialis Cultos (Pope Paul VI, Pauline Books and Media, Boston, Massachusetts, February 2, 1974). 56 pages.

The Dignity and Vocation of Women (Mulieris Dignitatem) (Pope John Paul II, Pauline Books and Media, Boston, Massachusetts, August 15, 1988).

Guardian of the Redeemer: On the Person and Mission of St. Joseph in the Life of Christ and of the Church— Redemptoris Custos (Pope John Paul II, Pauline Books and Media, Boston, Massachusetts, August 15, 1989).

In Joseph's Workshop (Blessed Josemaria Escriva, Scepter Booklets, Post Office Box 1270, Princeton, New Jersey 08543, 1975). 24 pages.

Jesus of Nazareth, video, 371 minutes, Ignatius Press, San Francisco, California.

Joseph: The Man Closest to Christ, video, 60 minutes, Ignatius Press, San Francisco, California.

Joseph in the New Testament (Fr. Larry M. Toschi, OSJ, Guardian of the Redeemer Books, 544 West Cliff Drive, Santa Cruz, California 95060, 1991). 156 pages.

Life with Joseph (Rev. Paul J. Gorman, The Leaflet Missal Company, 419 West Minnehaha Avenue, St. Paul, Minnesota 55103, 1988). 96 pages.

Mary: Mirror of the Church (Fr. Ramiero Cantalamessa, Ignatius Press, San Francisco, California). 214 pages.

Mary of Nazareth, video, 15 minutes, Ignatius Press, San Francisco, California.

Mission of the Redeemer (Redemptoris Missio) (Pope John Paul II, Pauline Books and Media, Boston, Massachusetts, December 7, 1990).

Mother of the Redeemer (Redemptoris Mater) On the Blessed Virgin Mary in the Life of the Pilgrim Church (Pope John Paul II, Pauline Books and Media, Boston, Massachusetts, March 25, 1987).

True Devotion to Mary (St. Louis-Marie Grignion de Montfort, translated by Fr. Frederick William Faber, Tan Books and Publisher, Inc., Post Office Box 424, Rock Cord, Illinois 61105, 1985). 215 pages.

The Vocation and Mission of Joseph and Mary (Paul Molinari, SJ and Anne Hennesy, CSJ, Veritas Publications, 7–8 Lower Abbey Street, Dublin 1, 1992). 59 pages.

Chapter 2—The Mission

Christian Fatherhood (Stephen Wood, Family Life Center Publications, Post Office Box 6060, Pt. Charlotte, FL 33949, 1997). 165 pages.

Full of Grace—Women and the Abundant Life (Johnnette Benkovic, Servant Publications, Ann Arbor, Michigan, 1998). 238 pages.

Letter to Families (Pope John Paul II, Pauline Books and Media, Boston, Massachusetts, February 2, 1994).

The New Wine Christian Witness of the Family (Cardinal Carlo Maria Martini, St. Paul Books and Media, Boston, Massachusetts, 1994). 319 pages.

The Role of the Christian Family in the Modern World—Familiaris Consortio (Pope John Paul II, Pauline Books and Media, Boston, Massachusetts, November 22, 1981).

Talking to Your Children about Being Catholic (Our Sunday Visitor; Inc., Huntington, Indiana, 1991). 141 pages.

The Truth and Meaning of Human Sexuality—Guidelines for Education Within the Family (Pontifical Council for the Family, St. Paul Books and Media, Boston, Massachusetts, 1996). 95 pages.

We Are on a Mission from God (Mary Beth Bonacci, Ignatius Press, San Francisco, California, 1996). 215 pages.

Chapter 3—The Journey

Bringing Christ's Presence Into Your Home—Your Family as a Domestic Church (Keith A. Fournier, Thomas Nelson Publishers, Nashville, Tennessee, 1992). 227 pages.

The Catholic Family Resource Guide (Barbara Meng and Rev. T. G. Morrow, Catholic Faith Alive!, Inc., 1910 Ventura Avenue, Silver Spring, Maryland, 20902, 1995). 112 pages.

Love and Family (Mercedes Arzu' Wilson, Ignatius Press, San Francisco, California, 1996). 383 pages.

Only Heroic Catholic Families Will Survive (Fr. Robert J. Fox, Family Apostolate, Post Office Box 55, Redfield, South Dakota 57469, 1994). 296 pages.

Parenting with Prayer (Mary Ann Kuharski, Our Sunday Visitor, Inc., Huntington, Indiana, 1993). 190 pages.

Raising Catholic Children (Mary Ann Kuharski, Our Sunday Visitor, Inc., Huntington, Indiana, 1991), 192 pages.

Speaking to the Heart—A Father's Guide to Growth in Virtue (Stephen Gabriel, Our Sunday Visitor, Huntington, Indiana, 1999). 136 pages.

The Vocation and Mission of the Lay Faithful in the Church and in the World—Christifideles Laici (Pope John Paul II, Pauline Books and Media, Boston, Massachusetts, December 30, 1988). 181 pages.

Chapter 4—The Path

Family Nights (or Days)

The Catholic Parent Book of Feasts (Michaelann Martin, Carol Puccio, and Zöe Romanowsky, Our Sunday Visitor, Huntington, Indiana, 1999). 192 pages.

Religious Instruction

Catechism of the Catholic Church. English translation of the *Catechism of the Catholic Church* for the United States of America, 1994, United States Catholic Conference, Inc., Libreria Editrice Vaticana.

Faith and Life Religion Series, Grades 1 to 8, Ignatius Press, San Francisco, California.

Education in Prayer

Prayers for Little Children, video, 30 minutes, Ignatius Press, San Francisco, California.

The Holy Eucharist

Adoration (Edited by Daniel Guersey, Ignatius Press, San Francisco, California, 1999). 250 pages.

I Am the Living Bread, video, 30 minutes, Ignatius Press, San Francisco, California.

Praying in the Presence of Our Lord (Fr. Benedict Groeschel, CFR, Our Sunday Visitor, Huntington, Indiana, 1999). 90 pages.

Transforming Your Life through the Eucharist (John Kane, Sophia Institute Press, Manchester, New Hampshire 03108). 167 pages.

The Holy Rosary for Families

The Essential Rosary (Caryll Houselander, Sophia Institute Press, Box 5284, Manchester, New Hampshire 03108, 1996). 86 pages.

The History and Devotion of the Rosary (Richard Gribble, SCS, Our Sunday Visitor Publishing Division, Huntington, Indiana 46750, 1992).

The Holy Rosary (Lawrence Lovasik, SVD, Catholic Book Publishing Company, New York 1980). Excellent book for young children and their parents.

I Can Pray the Rosary (Mary Terese Donze, Liguori Publications, One Liguori Drive Liguori, Missouri 63057, 1991; 314-464-2500). Excellent book for young children and their parents.

Praying the Rosary (Missionary Oblates of Mary Immaculate, Belleville, Illinois 62223, 1993).

The Rosary (Karen Cavanagh, CSJ, The Regina Press, New York, 1989). Excellent for young children and their parents.

The Rosary of Our Lady (Romano Guardini, Ignatius Press, San Francisco, California). 160 pages.

Rosary Prayer Book (Father Patrick Peyton, The Family Rosary, Inc., Albany, New York 1984).

The Scriptural Rosary (Christianica Center, Post Office Box 685, Glenview, Illinois 60025, 1989).

The Secret of the Rosary (St. Louis Mary De Montfort, Montfort Publications, Bay Shore, New York 11706, 1954).

Youth Prays the Rosary (Leaflet Missal Company, 976 West Minnehaha Avenue, St. Paul, Minnesota 55104, 1988).

Sacred Heart Enthronement

National Enthronement Center (3 Adams Street, Fairhaven, Massachusetts 02719).

Scripture Reading

God's Word Today (5615 West Cermak Road, Cicero, Illinois 60650). A program of daily scripture reading, commentary, and prayer.

Ignatius Bible. The Revised Standard Version—Catholic Edition. Ignatius Press.

Little Rock Scripture Study Program (Liturgical Press, Post Office Box 7500, Collegeville, Minnesota 56321, 1-800-858-5432). Materials specially designed for children and adults.

Read-Aloud Bible Stories, Vols. 1 to 4 (Moody Press, Chicago, Illinois). For preschool age; full-color illustrations.

Saints

The Book of Saints: The Lives of Saints According to the Liturgical Calendar (Regina Press, 1986).

Book of Saints, Parts 1–8 (Rev. Lawrence G. Lovasik, SVD, Catholic Book Publishing Company, New York, 1981–1993).

The Children's Book of Saints (The Regina Press, 145 Sherwood Avenue, Farmingdale, New York 11735, 1986).

Holy Traders Cards (Aziriah Company, P. O. Box 1986, Ft. Royal, Virginia 33630, 1-800-242-8467).

The One Year Book of Saints (Rev. Clifford Stevens, Our Sunday Visitor Publishing Division, Huntington, Indiana, 1989). 383 pages.

A Saint For Your Name. Boys and girls versions available (Our Sunday Visitor, Inc., Huntington, Indiana 46750, 1980).

Saints and Other Powerful Men in the Church (Bob and Penny Lord, Journeys of Faith, 1990). 527 pages.

Saints and Other Powerful Women in the Church (Bob and Penny Lord, Journeys of Faith, 1994). 396 pages.

The Saint's Kit (Loyola University Press, 3441 North Ashland Avenue, Chicago, Illinois 60657, 1-800-621-1008).

Vision Books Lives of the Saints Series (Numerous titles available from Ignatius Press, San Francisco, California).

Brown Scapular

Garment of Grace (Immaculate Heart Publications, Box 1028, Buffalo, New York 14205, 1-800-263-9160).

Scapulars (child and adult sizes) (Rose Scapular Company, 5203 Whitecap Street, Oxnard, California 93035).

Teaching Christian Virtues

Back to Virtue (Peter Kreeft, Ignatius Press, San Francisco, California, 1992). 195 pages.

The Book of Virtues (William J. Bennett, Simon and Schuster, New York, 1995). 824 pages.

The Book of Virtues for Young People (William J. Bennett, Silver Burdette Press, 299 Jefferson Road, Parsippany, New Jersey 07054, 1996). 384 pages.

Character Building (David Isaacs, Four Courts Press, Kill Lane, Black Rock, County Dublin, 1993), 262 pages.

The Heart of Virtue (Donald De Marco, Ignatius Press, San Francisco, California, 1996). 231 pages.

Learning the Virtues that Lead You to God (Romano Guardini, Ignatius Press, San Francisco, California). 214 pages.

The Moral Compass (William J. Bennett, Simon and Schuster, New York, 1995). 824 pages.

Story Telling

Catholic Digest Magazine (University of St. Thomas, 2115 Summit Avenue, St. Paul, Minnesota 55105).

Catholic Scouting

The Boy Scouts of America Family Book (Boy Scouts of America, Irving, Texas, 1990).

National Catholic Committee on Scouting, Boy Scouts of America (1325 West Walnut Hill Lane, Post Office Box 152079, Irving Texas 75015-2079, 1-214-580-2000).

National Catholic Committee for Girl Scouts and Camp Fire Boys and Girls (3700-A Oakview Terrace, NE, Washington, DC 20017-2591, 1-202-636-3825).

Fostering Vocations and Lifework Choices

LifeWork: Finding Your Purpose in Life (Rick Sarkisian, Ph.D., Ignatius Press, San Francisco, California, 1997). 123 pages.

LifeWork: Finding God's Purpose for Your Life, video, 45 minutes, Ignatius Press, San Francisco, California.

Chapter 5—The Destination

Appointment with God (Michael Scanlan, TOR, Franciscan University Press, Steubenville, Ohio, 1987). 57 pages.

*Catholic Household Blessings and
Prayers* (Bishops Committee
on the Liturgy/National
Conference of Catholic
Bishops, The Liturgical Press,
St. John's Abbey, Collegeville,
Minnesota 56321, 1988).
434 pages.

*Guiltless Catholic Parenting from
A to Y* (Bert Ghezzi, Servant
Publications, Post Office Box
8617, Ann Arbor, Michigan
48107, 1995). 270 pages.

*A Prayer Book for Young
Catholics* (Fr. Robert J. Fox,
Our Sunday Visitor, Inc., 200
Noll Plaza, Huntington,
Indiana 46750, 1981).
168 pages.

Prayer: The Great Conversation
(Peter Kreeft, Ignatius Press,
San Francisco, California,
1991). 178 pages.

*Prayers, Activities, Celebrations
(and More) for Catholic
Families* (Bridget Mary
Meehan, Twenty-Third
Publications, 185 Willow St.,
Mystic, Connecticut 06355,
1995). 69 pages.

*Upbringing: a Discussion
Handbook for Parents of
Young Children* (James B.
Stenson, Scepter Publishers,
Inc., Princeton, New Jersey,
1991). 176 pages.

Magazines

The following magazines are
highly recommended. (Reviews
are by Patrick Madrid, Editor of
ENVOY Magazine, 1998)

Our Sunday Visitor

Week after week, *Our Sunday
Visitor* offers an exciting and
relevant mix of hard news,
feature articles, opinion pieces,
human interest stories, and a lot
more. You get a trustworthy,
balanced view of the Church
from a uniquely American perspective. *OSV* is faithful to the
Pope and the Magisterium but
always challenging and hard-hit-
ting in its journalism. Call
800-348-2440, 200 Noll Plaza
Huntington, Indiana 46750.

National Catholic Register

The *National Catholic Register*
consistently delivers a wide
range of breaking Catholic news
and incisive editorials. Its quick-
read, in-depth format taps deep
into the vitality of the Church
and equips readers to engage
the emerging culture. Call
800-421-3230, or write to P.O.
Box 373, Mt. Morris, Illinois
61054.

New Covenant

New Covenant features today's top Catholic writers, compelling articles and excellent graphics to boot. Call 800-348-2440, 200 Noll Plaza Huntington, Indiana 46750.

Catholic Faith & Family

An inspiring and practical weekly for parents who want to build their family life on the rock of the Catholic Faith. Each issue brims with enjoyable, pertinent feature stories and sound advice on parenting and marital issues. 800-421-3230, P. O. Box 369, Mt. Morris, Illinois 61054.

ZENIT News Agency

The ZENIT News Agency is a relatively new Internet news service based in Rome, the very heart of the Catholic Church. ZENIT's international journalists and Vatican insiders provide a unique blend of Catholic news you can't get elsewhere. Subscriptions are free. Visit www.zenit.org or send an e-mail to English-request@Zenit.org and add the word "subscribe" in the subject field.

Mission Statement

_____

_____

_____

_____

_____

_____

_____

_____

_____

_____

_____

_____

_____

_____

_____

_____

Signed by:

_____   _____

_____   _____

_____   _____

_____   _____

_____
Date